COPPER SKILLET
Cooking

Publications International, Ltd.

Pictured on the front cover: Easy Chicken Parmesan *(page 64)*.
Pictured on the back cover *(left to right):* Poached Pears in Cinnamon-Apricot Sauce *(page 102)*, Crispy Buttermilk Fried Chicken *(page 72)* and Caramelized Brussels Sprouts with Cranberries *(page 80)*.

ISBN: 978-1-68022-796-3

Library of Congress Control Number: 2016958004

Manufactured in China.

8 7 6 5 4 3 2 1

Microwave Cooking: Microwave ovens vary in wattage. Use the cooking times as guidelines and check for doneness before adding more time.

TABLE OF
Contents

BREAKFAST & BRUNCH

Cranberry Buttermilk Pancakes

1 cup all-purpose flour

1 cup whole wheat flour

2 teaspoons baking powder

1 teaspoon baking soda

½ teaspoon ground cinnamon

¼ teaspoon ground nutmeg

⅔ cup whole berry cranberry sauce, divided

2 eggs

2 tablespoons vegetable oil

1½ cups buttermilk

Maple syrup (optional)

1. Combine all-purpose flour, whole wheat flour, baking powder, baking soda, cinnamon and nutmeg in small bowl; mix well. Whisk cranberry sauce, eggs and oil in large bowl until well blended. Gradually stir in flour mixture until combined. Stir in buttermilk until smooth and well blended.

2. Heat large skillet over medium heat. Pour ¼ cupfuls of batter 2 inches apart into skillet; cook 3 minutes or until lightly browned and edges begin to bubble. Turn over; cook 3 minutes or until lightly browned. Repeat with remaining batter. Serve with syrup, if desired.

MAKES 18 (3-INCH) PANCAKES

Ham and Vegetable Omelet

1 tablespoon vegetable oil

2 ounces (about ½ cup) diced ham

1 small onion, diced

½ medium green bell pepper, diced

½ medium red bell pepper, diced

2 cloves garlic, minced

6 eggs

⅛ teaspoon black pepper

½ cup (2 ounces) shredded Colby cheese, divided

1 medium tomato, chopped

Hot pepper sauce (optional)

1. Heat oil in large skillet over medium-high heat. Add ham, onion, bell peppers and garlic; cook and stir 5 minutes or until vegetables are crisp-tender. Remove mixture to large bowl.

2. Return skillet to medium-high heat. Pour eggs into skillet; sprinkle with black pepper. Cook 2 minutes or until bottom is set, lifting edge of egg with spatula to allow uncooked portion to flow underneath. Reduce heat to medium-low; cover and cook 4 minutes or until top is set.

3. Gently slide omelet onto large serving plate; spoon ham mixture down center. Sprinkle with ¼ cup cheese. Carefully fold two sides of omelet over ham mixture; sprinkle with remaining ¼ cup cheese and tomato. Cut into four wedges; serve immediately with hot pepper sauce, if desired.

MAKES 4 SERVINGS

Andouille Sausage Cajun Scramble

½ package (13.5 ounces) JOHNSONVILLE® Andouille Fully Cooked Sausage

6 large eggs, beaten

1 teaspoon Cajun seasoning

2 to 3 tablespoons olive oil

1 small red potato, cut into ¼-inch dice

1 small onion, chopped

½ cup chopped green bell pepper

½ cup shredded pepper jack cheese

½ cup salsa (optional)

1. Cut sausage link diagonally into ¼-inch slices; set aside. Whisk together eggs and Cajun seasoning in medium bowl; set aside.

2. Heat 2 tablespoons oil in large nonstick skillet over medium-low heat until hot. Add potato; cook and stir 5 minutes. Increase heat to medium. Add onion and bell pepper; cook and stir 5 minutes or until vegetables are lightly browned. Add sausage slices; cook and stir 2 to 3 minutes. If skillet seems dry, add remaining 1 tablespoon oil and heat.

3. Pour egg mixture into skillet; cook without stirring 1 minute. Gently bring edges of mixture to center, allowing uncooked egg mixture to reach pan bottom. Continue cooking and folding to blend ingredients. When eggs are still moist but almost cooked through, add cheese. Cook and fold 30 to 45 seconds or until cheese has melted.

4. Divide evenly between two plates; top evenly with salsa, if desired. Serve immediately.

MAKES 2 SERVINGS

Turkey Bacon Mini Wafflewiches

1 teaspoon Dijon mustard

1 teaspoon honey

8 frozen mini waffles
(2 pieces, divided
into individual waffles)

2 thin slices deli turkey,
cut into thin strips

2 tablespoons cooked
and crumbled bacon

4 teaspoons shredded
Cheddar or mozzarella
cheese

2 teaspoons butter

1. Combine mustard and honey in small bowl. Spread small amount of mustard mixture onto one side of 4 waffles. Top evenly with turkey and bacon; sprinkle with cheese. Top with 4 remaining waffles.

2. Heat butter in large skillet over medium heat. Pressing with back of spatula, cook sandwiches 3 to 4 minutes per side or until cheese is melted and waffles are golden brown.

MAKES 2 SERVINGS

Fire & Ice Brunch Skillet

1 (6.8-ounce) package RICE-A-RONI® Spanish Rice

2 tablespoons margarine or butter

1 (16-ounce) jar salsa

⅓ cup sour cream

¼ cup thinly sliced green onions

4 large eggs

1 cup (4 ounces) shredded Cheddar cheese

Chopped cilantro (optional)

1. In large skillet over medium heat, sauté rice-vermicelli mix with margarine until vermicelli is golden brown.

2. Slowly stir in 2 cups water, salsa and Special Seasonings; bring to a boil. Reduce heat to low. Cover; simmer 15 to 20 minutes or until rice is tender.

3. Stir in sour cream and green onions. Using large spoon, make 4 indentations in rice mixture. Break 1 egg into each indentation. Reduce heat to low. Cover; cook 8 minutes or until eggs are cooked to desired doneness.

4. Sprinkle cheese evenly over eggs and rice. Cover; let stand 3 minutes or until cheese is melted. Sprinkle with cilantro, if desired.

MAKES 4 SERVINGS

Tip: A twist on Mexican-style huevos rancheros, serve this for brunch or as a light dinner.

Skillet Sausage with Potatoes and Rosemary

1 tablespoon vegetable oil

3 cups diced red skin potatoes

1 cup diced onion

1 pound BOB EVANS® Original Recipe Roll Sausage

½ teaspoon dried rosemary

¼ teaspoon rubbed sage

Salt and black pepper to taste

2 tablespoons chopped fresh parsley

Heat oil in large skillet over medium-high heat 1 minute. Add potatoes; cook 5 to 10 minutes or until slightly brown, stirring occasionally. Add onion; cook until tender. Add crumbled sausage; cook until browned. Add rosemary, sage, salt and pepper; cook and stir until well blended. Transfer to serving platter and garnish with parsley. Refrigerate leftovers.

MAKES 4 TO 6 SERVINGS

Mexed-Up French Toast with Spiced Chocolate Drizzle

6 eggs, beaten

½ cup half-and-half or milk

1 packet (1.25 ounces) ORTEGA® Taco Seasoning Mix or 40% Less Sodium Taco Seasoning Mix, divided

8 slices Texas toast-style bread, thawed if frozen

2 tablespoons butter

1 cup semisweet chocolate chips

¼ cup whipping cream

Maple Grove Farms® maple syrup

COMBINE eggs, half-and-half and 2 tablespoons seasoning mix in shallow bowl or pie pan; mix well.

PLACE bread slices in egg mixture, allowing bread to absorb mixture before turning to coat other side.

HEAT about ½ tablespoon butter in large skillet over medium heat. Place 2 egg-coated bread slices in skillet; cook about 4 minutes or until golden brown. Turn slices over and cook 4 minutes or until golden brown. Transfer to serving plate. Repeat with remaining butter and bread slices.

PLACE chocolate chips and remaining seasoning mix in small microwavable bowl. Microwave on HIGH 30 seconds; stir. Repeat as necessary until chips are melted and mixture is smooth. Stir in cream; mix well.

DRIZZLE chocolate mixture over French toast and serve with maple syrup.

MAKES 4 SERVINGS

Sweet Potato and Turkey Sausage Hash

1 mild or hot turkey Italian sausage link (about 4 ounces)

1 tablespoon vegetable oil

1 small red onion, finely chopped

1 small red bell pepper, finely chopped

1 small sweet potato, peeled and cut into ½-inch cubes

¼ teaspoon salt (optional)

¼ teaspoon black pepper

⅛ teaspoon ground cumin

⅛ teaspoon chipotle chili powder

1. Remove sausage from casings; discard. Shape sausage into ½-inch balls. Heat oil in large skillet over medium heat. Add sausage; cook and stir 3 to 5 minutes or until browned. Remove from skillet; set aside.

2. Add onion, bell pepper, sweet potato, salt, if desired, black pepper, cumin and chili powder; cook and stir 5 to 8 minutes or until sweet potato is tender.

3. Stir in sausage; cook without stirring 5 minutes or until hash is lightly browned.

MAKES 2 SERVINGS

Sausage and Red Pepper Strata

6 ounces bulk breakfast pork sausage

½ teaspoon dried oregano

¼ teaspoon red pepper flakes (optional)

4 slices day-old French bread, cut into ½-inch cubes

½ medium red bell pepper, finely chopped

¼ cup chopped fresh parsley, plus additional for garnish

4 eggs

1 cup evaporated milk

1 teaspoon Dijon mustard

¼ teaspoon black pepper

½ cup (2 ounces) shredded sharp Cheddar cheese

1. Heat large skillet over medium-high heat. Add sausage, oregano and red pepper flakes, if desired; cook and stir 6 to 8 minutes or until sausage is browned, stirring to break up meat. Drain fat. Remove mixture to large bowl.

2. Line bottom of skillet with bread cubes. Sprinkle sausage mixture evenly over bread cubes; top evenly with bell pepper and ¼ cup parsley. Whisk eggs, evaporated milk, mustard and black pepper in medium bowl until well blended. Pour egg mixture over sausage. Cover tightly with foil; refrigerate 8 hours or overnight.

3. Preheat oven to 350°F. Bake, covered, 55 minutes.

4. Remove foil. Sprinkle with cheese; bake 5 minutes or until cheese is melted. Garnish with additional parsley. Cut into four pieces before serving.

MAKES 4 SERVINGS

Apple Monte Cristos

4 ounces Gouda cheese, shredded

1 ounce cream cheese, softened

2 teaspoons honey

½ teaspoon ground cinnamon

4 slices cinnamon raisin bread

1 small apple, cored and thinly sliced

¼ cup milk

1 egg, beaten

1 tablespoon butter

Powdered sugar

1. Combine Gouda cheese, cream cheese, honey and cinnamon in small bowl; stir until well blended. Spread cheese mixture evenly on all bread slices. Layer apple slices evenly over cheese on 2 bread slices; top with remaining bread slices.

2. Combine milk and egg in shallow bowl; stir until well blended. Dip sandwiches in egg mixture, turning to coat well.

3. Melt butter in large skillet over medium heat. Add sandwiches; cook 4 to 5 minutes per side or until cheese is melted and sandwiches are golden brown. Sprinkle with powdered sugar.

MAKES 2 SANDWICHES

Tip: Melting the butter in the skillet before adding the sandwiches, adds additional buttery flavor.

Turkey Migas

10 large eggs

1 teaspoon chili powder

¼ cup (½ stick) butter

1 cup onion, cut into 1½×¼-inch strips

1 cup green bell pepper, cut into 1½×¼-inch strips

1 cup red bell pepper, cut into 1½×¼-inch strips

2 cups diced leftover cooked BUTTERBALL® Turkey

1 cup (4 ounces) shredded pepper jack cheese

4 ounces corn chips

20 fresh cilantro leaves

1 cup prepared chunky salsa

1. Beat eggs with chili powder in medium bowl; set aside.

2. Melt butter in medium skillet over medium-high heat. Add onion and bell peppers; cook and stir 2 to 3 minutes or until crisp-tender.

3. Add turkey and egg mixture; stir well. Reduce heat to medium. When eggs begin to set, draw heatproof spatula along bottom and sides of skillet to loosen eggs. Stir in cheese. Continue to loosen cooked eggs from bottom and sides of skillet. Gently fold in corn chips. Continue cooking until egg mixture is set.

4. Spoon onto serving platter. Sprinkle with cilantro; pour salsa down center.

MAKES 6 SERVINGS

Pea and Spinach Frittata

1 cup chopped onion

¼ cup water

1 cup frozen peas

1 cup fresh spinach

6 egg whites

2 eggs

½ cup cooked brown rice

¼ cup milk

2 tablespoons grated Romano or Parmesan cheese, plus additional for garnish

1 tablespoon chopped fresh mint *or* 1 teaspoon dried mint

¼ teaspoon black pepper

⅛ teaspoon salt

1. Combine onion and water in skillet. Bring to a boil over high heat. Reduce heat to medium. Cover and cook 2 to 3 minutes or until onion is tender. Stir in peas; cook until heated through. Drain. Add spinach; cook and stir 1 minute or until spinach just begins to wilt.

2. Combine egg whites, eggs, rice, milk, 2 tablespoons Romano cheese, mint, pepper and salt in medium bowl. Add egg mixture to skillet. Cook, without stirring, 2 minutes until eggs begin to set. Run large spoon around edge of skillet, lifting eggs for even cooking. Remove skillet from heat when eggs are almost set but surface is still moist.

3. Cover; let stand 3 to 4 minutes or until surface is set. Sprinkle with additional Romano cheese, if desired. Cut into four wedges to serve.

MAKES 4 SERVINGS

Ham and Potato Pancakes

¾ pound Yukon Gold potatoes, peeled, grated and squeezed dry (about 2 cups)

¼ cup finely chopped green onions

2 eggs, beaten

1 cup (4 to 5 ounces) finely chopped cooked ham

¼ cup rice flour

¼ teaspoon salt

¼ teaspoon black pepper

3 tablespoons vegetable oil

Chili sauce or fruit chutney (optional)

1. Combine potatoes, green onions and eggs in large bowl; mix well. Add ham, rice flour, salt and pepper; mix well.

2. Heat 2 tablespoons oil in large skillet over medium-high heat. Drop batter into skillet by heaping tablespoonfuls and press with back of spoon to flatten. Cook 2 to 3 minutes per side. Remove to paper towels to drain. Add remaining 1 tablespoon oil, if necessary, to cook remaining batter. Serve pancakes with chili sauce.

MAKES 16 PANCAKES

Tip: Rice flour can often be substituted for regular all-purpose flour in recipes like this one. If a small amount of flour is called for to bind ingredients together, rice flour works just as well as regular flour. Use either brown or white rice flour. Brown rice flour, like the brown rice it is made from, has a slightly better nutritional profile.

APPETIZERS & SNACKS

Mac & Cheese Bites

3 packages (3 ounces each) ramen noodles, any flavor, divided*

8 ounces pasteurized process cheese product

1 cup (4 ounces) shredded Cheddar cheese

1 teaspoon salt

½ teaspoon ground red pepper

Vegetable oil

*Discard seasoning packets.

1. Prepare 2 packages ramen according to package directions; drain and return to saucepan.

2. Stir in cheese product, Cheddar cheese, salt and ground red pepper. Let stand 10 to 15 minutes.

3. Finely crush remaining packet ramen noodles in food processor or blender. Put crumbs in pie pan. Using hands, shape cheese mixture into 1-inch balls; roll in ramen crumbs. Flatten slightly.

4. Heat about ½ to 1 inch oil in large skillet. Add bites, a few at a time; cook 1½ minutes per side until golden brown. Remove from skillet; drain on paper towels.

MAKES ABOUT 2 DOZEN BITES

Elegant Shrimp Scampi

¼ cup (½ stick) plus 2 tablespoons butter

6 to 8 cloves garlic, minced

1½ pounds large raw shrimp (about 16), peeled and deveined (with tails on)

6 green onions, thinly sliced

¼ cup dry white wine

Juice of 1 lemon (about 2 tablespoons)

¼ cup chopped fresh parsley

Salt and black pepper

Lemon slices (optional)

1. Clarify butter by melting it in large skillet over low heat. *Do not stir.* Skim off white foam that forms on top. Strain clarified butter through cheesecloth into glass measuring cup to yield ⅓ cup. Discard cheesecloth and milky residue at bottom of skillet.

2. Heat clarified butter in large skillet over medium heat. Add garlic; cook and stir 1 to 2 minutes or until softened but not browned.

3. Add shrimp, green onions, wine and lemon juice; cook and stir 3 to 4 minutes or until shrimp are pink and opaque. *Do not overcook.*

4. Stir in parsley and season with salt and pepper. Garnish with lemon slices.

MAKES 8 SERVINGS

Spicy BBQ Party Franks

1 tablespoon butter

1 package (1 pound) cocktail franks

⅓ cup COCA-COLA®

⅓ cup ketchup

2 tablespoons hot pepper sauce

1 tablespoon cider vinegar

2 tablespoons packed dark brown sugar

Heat butter in medium skillet over medium heat. Pierce cocktail franks with fork. Add franks to skillet and brown slightly.

Pour in *Coca-Cola*, ketchup, hot pepper sauce and vinegar. Stir in brown sugar; reduce heat.

Cook until sticky glaze is achieved. Serve with toothpicks.

MAKES 6 TO 8 SERVINGS

Quesadilla Grande

2 (8-inch) flour tortillas

2 to 3 large fresh stemmed spinach leaves

2 to 3 slices (about 3 ounces) cooked boneless skinless chicken breast

2 tablespoons salsa

1 tablespoon chopped fresh cilantro

¼ cup (1 ounce) shredded Monterey Jack cheese

2 teaspoons butter or margarine (optional)

1. Place 1 tortilla in large skillet; cover tortilla with spinach leaves. Place chicken in single layer over spinach. Spoon salsa over chicken. Sprinkle with cilantro; top with cheese. Place remaining tortilla on top, pressing tortilla down so filling becomes compact.

2. Cook over medium heat 4 to 5 minutes or until bottom tortilla is lightly browned. Holding top tortilla in place, gently turn over. Continue cooking 4 minutes or until bottom tortilla is browned and cheese is melted.

3. For a crispier finish, place butter in skillet to melt; lift quesadilla to let butter flow into center of skillet. Cook 30 seconds. Turn over; continue cooking 30 seconds. Cut into wedges to serve.

MAKES 1 SERVING

Mini Beef Albóndigas

1 pound Ground Beef

¼ cup soft whole wheat bread crumbs

1 large egg, slightly beaten

4 tablespoons chopped fresh cilantro, divided

1 teaspoon ground chipotle chili powder, divided

½ teaspoon salt

1 can (15 ounces) tomato sauce

2 tablespoons water

Chopped fresh cilantro (optional)

1. Combine Ground Beef, bread crumbs, egg, 2 tablespoons cilantro, ½ teaspoon chipotle chili powder and salt in large bowl, mixing lightly but thoroughly. Shape into 24 one-inch meatballs. Heat large nonstick skillet over medium heat until hot. Place meatballs in skillet; cook 8 minutes or until browned on all sides.

2. Add tomato sauce, water, remaining 2 tablespoons cilantro and remaining ½ teaspoon chipotle chili powder; bring to a boil. Reduce heat. Cover and simmer 8 to 10 minutes, stirring once.

3. Serve meatballs on skewers or on platter with toothpicks. Sprinkle with cilantro, if desired.

MAKES 12 SERVINGS

Courtesy of The Beef Checkoff

Spicy Chicken Bundles

1 pound ground chicken

2 teaspoons minced fresh ginger

2 cloves garlic, minced

¼ teaspoon red pepper flakes

3 tablespoons soy sauce

1 tablespoon cornstarch

1 tablespoon peanut or vegetable oil

⅓ cup finely chopped water chestnuts

⅓ cup thinly sliced green onions

¼ cup chopped peanuts

12 large lettuce leaves, such as romaine

Chinese hot mustard (optional)

1. Combine chicken, ginger, garlic and red pepper flakes in medium bowl. Blend soy sauce into cornstarch in cup until smooth.

2. Heat oil in large skillet over medium-high heat. Add chicken mixture; cook and stir 2 to 3 minutes until chicken is cooked through.

3. Stir soy sauce mixture; add to skillet. Stir-fry 30 seconds or until sauce boils and thickens. Add water chestnuts, green onions and peanuts; heat through.*

4. Divide filling evenly among lettuce leaves; roll up. Secure with toothpicks. Serve warm or at room temperature. Do not let filling stand at room temperature more than 2 hours. Serve with hot mustard.

MAKES 12 APPETIZERS

Filling may be made ahead to this point; cover and refrigerate up to 4 hours. Reheat chicken filling until warm. Proceed as directed in step 4.

Shrimp Tapas in Sherry Sauce

1 slice thick-cut bacon, cut crosswise into ¼-inch strips

2 ounces cremini or button mushrooms, cut into quarters

½ pound large raw shrimp (about 16), peeled and deveined (with tails on)

2 cloves garlic, thinly sliced

2 tablespoons medium dry sherry

1 tablespoon fresh lemon juice

¼ teaspoon red pepper flakes

1. Cook bacon in large skillet over medium heat until crisp. Remove from skillet with slotted spoon; drain on paper towels. Set aside.

2. Add mushrooms to bacon drippings; cook and stir 2 minutes. Add shrimp and garlic; cook and stir 3 minutes or until shrimp turn pink and opaque. Stir in sherry, lemon juice and red pepper flakes. Remove shrimp to serving bowl with slotted spoon.

3. Cook sauce 1 minute or until reduced and thickened. Pour over shrimp. Sprinkle with bacon.

MAKES 4 SERVINGS

Falafel Nuggets

- 2 cans (about 15 ounces each) chickpeas
- ½ cup whole wheat flour
- ½ cup chopped fresh parsley
- 1 egg, beaten
- ⅓ cup lemon juice
- ¼ cup minced onion
- 2 tablespoons minced garlic
- 2 teaspoons ground cumin
- ½ teaspoon salt
- ½ teaspoon ground red pepper or red pepper flakes
- Nonstick cooking spray
- Marinara sauce

1. Preheat oven to 400°F.

2. Drain chickpeas, reserving ¼ cup liquid. Combine chickpeas, reserved ¼ cup liquid, flour, parsley, lemon juice, onion, garlic, cumin, salt and ground red pepper in food processor or blender; process until well blended. Shape into 36 (1-inch) balls; place 1 to 2 inches apart in large skillet. Refrigerate 15 minutes.

3. Remove skillet from refrigerator. Spray balls lightly with cooking spray. Bake 15 to 20 minutes, turning once. Serve with warm marinara sauce.

MAKES 12 SERVINGS

Beer Batter Tempura

1½ cups all-purpose flour

1½ cups Japanese beer, chilled

1 teaspoon salt

Dipping Sauce (recipe follows)

Vegetable oil for frying

½ pound green beans or asparagus tips

1 large sweet potato, cut into ¼-inch slices

1 medium eggplant, cut into ¼-inch slices

1. Combine flour, beer and salt in medium bowl just until mixed. Batter should be thin and lumpy. *Do not overmix.* Let stand 15 minutes. Meanwhile, prepare Dipping Sauce.

2. Heat 1 inch oil in large skillet to 375°F; adjust heat to maintain temperature.

3. Dip 10 to 12 green beans in batter; add to hot oil. Fry until light golden brown. Remove to wire racks or paper towels to drain; keep warm. Repeat with remaining vegetables, working with only one vegetable at a time and being careful not to crowd vegetables. Serve with Dipping Sauce.

MAKES 4 SERVINGS

Dipping Sauce

½ cup soy sauce

2 tablespoons rice wine

1 tablespoon sugar

½ teaspoon white vinegar

2 teaspoons minced fresh ginger

1 clove garlic, minced

2 green onions, thinly sliced

Combine soy sauce, rice wine, sugar and vinegar in small saucepan; cook and stir over medium heat 3 minutes or until sugar dissolves. Add ginger and garlic; cook and stir 2 minutes. Stir in green onions; remove from heat.

MAKES ABOUT 1 CUP

Toasted Monkey Sandwiches

¼ cup SKIPPY® Creamy
   Peanut Butter

4 slices cinnamon raisin,
   white or whole wheat
   bread

1 medium banana, sliced

1. Evenly spread SKIPPY® Creamy Peanut Butter on 2 slices bread, then top with banana and remaining bread slices.

2. Cook sandwiches in 12-inch nonstick skillet sprayed with nonstick cooking spray over medium heat until golden brown, about 4 minutes, turning once.

MAKES 2 SERVINGS

Tip: Try with Skippy® Natural Creamy Peanut Butter Spread with Honey!

Chicken Nuggets with Spicy Tomato Dipping Sauce

Spicy Tomato Dipping Sauce (recipe follows)

½ cup panko bread crumbs

½ cup grated Parmesan cheese

1 package (3 ounces) ramen noodles, any flavor, finely crushed*

1 teaspoon garlic powder

1 teaspoon dried basil

½ teaspoon salt

¼ teaspoon black pepper

1 egg, lightly beaten

1½ pounds boneless skinless chicken breasts, cut into 1×2½-inch pieces

½ cup vegetable oil

*Discard seasoning packet.

1. Prepare Spicy Tomato Dipping Sauce; set aside. Combine panko, cheese, noodles, garlic powder, basil, salt and pepper in large bowl. Place egg in shallow dish. Dip chicken in egg; shake off excess. Coat with panko mixture.

2. Heat oil in large skillet over medium heat. Cook chicken in batches about 5 minutes or until cooked through, turning once. Serve with Spicy Tomato Dipping Sauce.

MAKES 4 SERVINGS

Spicy Tomato Dipping Sauce

1 tablespoon olive oil

1 small onion, chopped

2 cloves garlic, minced

¼ teaspoon ground red pepper

1 can (about 14 ounces) fire-roasted diced tomatoes

1. Heat oil in medium skillet. Add onion and garlic; cook and stir about 3 minutes or until onion is tender and golden brown. Stir in ground red pepper.

2. Remove skillet from heat; add tomatoes. Process in blender or food processor until smooth. Return to skillet and cook about 10 minutes or until thickened and reduced to 1½ cups.

MAKES 1½ CUPS

DINNERTIME FAVORITES

Emerald Isle Lamb Chops

2 tablespoons vegetable or olive oil, divided

2 tablespoons coarse Dijon mustard

1 tablespoon Irish whiskey

1 tablespoon minced fresh rosemary

2 teaspoons minced garlic

1½ pounds loin lamb chops (about 6 chops)

½ teaspoon salt

½ teaspoon black pepper

¾ cup dry white wine

2 tablespoons black currant jam

1 to 2 tablespoons butter, cut into small pieces

1. Combine 1 tablespoon oil, mustard, whiskey, rosemary and garlic in small bowl to form paste. Season lamb chops with salt and pepper; spread paste over both sides. Cover and marinate 30 minutes at room temperature or refrigerate 2 to 3 hours.

2. Heat remaining 1 tablespoon oil in large skillet over medium-high heat. Add lamb chops in single layer; cook 2 to 3 minutes per side or until desired doneness. Remove to serving plate and keep warm.

3. Drain excess fat from skillet. Add wine; cook and stir about 5 minutes, scraping up brown bits from bottom of skillet. Stir in jam until well blended. Remove from heat; stir in butter until melted. Serve sauce over lamb chops.

MAKES 4 TO 6 SERVINGS

Pan-Fried Cajun Bass

2 tablespoons all-purpose flour

1 to 1½ teaspoons Cajun or Caribbean jerk seasoning

1 egg white

2 teaspoons water

⅓ cup seasoned dry bread crumbs

2 tablespoons cornmeal

4 skinless striped bass, halibut or cod fillets (4 to 6 ounces each), thawed if frozen

1 teaspoon butter

1 teaspoon olive oil

Chopped fresh parsley (optional)

4 lemon wedges

1. Combine flour and seasoning in medium resealable food storage bag. Beat egg white and water in small bowl. Combine bread crumbs and cornmeal in separate small bowl.

2. Working one at a time, add fillet to bag; shake to coat evenly. Dip in egg white mixture, letting excess drip back into bowl. Roll in bread crumb mixture, pressing lightly to adhere. Repeat with remaining fillets.

3. Melt butter and oil in large skillet over medium heat. Add fillets; cook 4 to 5 minutes per side or until golden brown and fish is opaque in center and flakes easily when tested with fork.

4. Sprinkle parsley over fish, if desired. Serve with lemon wedges.

MAKES 4 SERVINGS

Chicken and Chile Stir-Fry

½ cup orange juice

4½ teaspoons oyster sauce

1 tablespoon minced fresh ginger

1 teaspoon cornstarch

12 ounces boneless skinless chicken breasts, thinly sliced

4 ounces (about 6) jalapeño peppers,* stemmed, seeded and thinly sliced (½ cup)

4 ounces (about 3) poblano chile peppers, stemmed, seeded and thinly sliced (¾ cup)

8 cloves garlic, thinly sliced (2 tablespoons)

1 teaspoon olive oil

¼ cup slivered fresh basil or mint leaves

3 cups hot cooked rice

*Jalapeño and other peppers can sting and irritate the skin, so wear rubber gloves when handling peppers and do not touch your eyes.

1. Blend orange juice, oyster sauce and ginger into cornstarch in small bowl; set aside.

2. Heat large skillet over medium-high heat. Add half the chicken; stir-fry 4 minutes or until chicken is no longer pink in center. Remove; set aside. Repeat with remaining chicken.

3. Add jalapeño peppers, poblano peppers, garlic and oil to same skillet; reduce heat to medium. Cook, partially covered, 8 minutes, stirring often, or until peppers are tender. Return chicken to skillet. Add orange juice mixture. Cook and stir until sauce boils and thickens slightly. Remove from heat; stir in basil. Serve over rice.

MAKES 4 SERVINGS

Note: To add a subtle smoky flavor, roast jalapeño and poblano peppers. When peppers are cool enough to handle, peel skin and chop.

Veggie-Packed Spaghetti & Meatballs

4 ounces uncooked spaghetti or vermicelli

¾ pound lean ground turkey or beef

1 package (10 ounces) frozen chopped spinach, thawed and pressed dry

½ cup fresh whole wheat bread crumbs*

1 egg white

1 teaspoon onion powder

1 teaspoon garlic powder

½ teaspoon black pepper

Nonstick cooking spray

2 cups pasta sauce

2 cups (5 ounces) small broccoli florets

½ cup packaged julienned carrots

*To make fresh bread crumbs, tear 1 slice bread into pieces; process in food processor until coarse crumbs form.

1. Cook spaghetti according to package directions, omitting salt. Drain.

2. Meanwhile, combine turkey, spinach, bread crumbs, egg white, onion powder, garlic powder and pepper in medium bowl; mix well. Shape into 32 (½-inch) meatballs.

3. Heat large skillet over medium heat. Add meatballs; cook 8 to 10 minutes, turning to brown all sides.

4. Add pasta sauce, broccoli and carrots to skillet. Cover; bring to a simmer over medium-low heat. Cook 8 to 10 or until vegetables are tender and sauce is heated through.

5. Spoon sauce and meatballs evenly over spaghetti.

MAKES 4 SERVINGS

Salsa Bacon Burgers with Guacamole

1 pound ground beef

1 packet (1.25 ounces) ORTEGA® Taco Seasoning Mix

¼ cup ORTEGA® Salsa, any variety

2 ripe avocados

1 packet (1 ounce) ORTEGA® Guacamole Seasoning Mix

4 hamburger buns

8 slices cooked bacon

COMBINE ground beef, taco seasoning mix and salsa in large mixing bowl. With clean hands, form meat mixture into 4 patties.

CUT avocados in half and remove pits. Scoop out avocado meat and smash in small bowl. Add guacamole seasoning mix. Set aside.

HEAT large skillet over medium heat; cook burgers 5 minutes. Flip burgers and continue to cook another 7 minutes.

PLACE burgers on bottom of buns. Top each burger with dollop of guacamole, 2 slices bacon and top bun.

MAKES 4 BURGERS

Tip: Make burgers half the size to create great sliders.

Pumpkin Curry

1 tablespoon vegetable oil

1 package (14 ounces) extra firm tofu, drained and cut into 1-inch cubes

¼ cup Thai red curry paste

2 cloves garlic, minced

1 can (15 ounces) solid-pack pumpkin

1 can (14 ounces) coconut milk

1 cup water

1½ teaspoons salt

1 teaspoon sriracha sauce

4 cups cut-up vegetables (broccoli, cauliflower, red bell pepper, sweet potato)

½ cup peas

2 cups hot cooked rice

¼ cup shredded fresh basil (optional)

1. Heat oil in large skillet over high heat. Add tofu; stir-fry 2 to 3 minutes or until lightly browned. Add curry paste and garlic; cook and stir 1 minute or until tofu is coated. Add pumpkin, coconut milk, water, salt and sriracha; bring to a boil. Stir in vegetables.

2. Reduce heat to medium; cover and simmer 20 minutes or until vegetables are tender. Stir in peas; cook 1 minute or until heated through. Serve over rice; top with basil, if desired.

MAKES 4 SERVINGS

Blackened Shrimp with Tomatoes

1½ teaspoons paprika

1 teaspoon Italian seasoning

½ teaspoon garlic powder

¼ teaspoon black pepper

½ pound (about 24) small raw shrimp, peeled (with tails on)

1 tablespoon canola oil

½ cup sliced red onion, separated into rings

1½ cups halved grape tomatoes

Lime wedges (optional)

1. Combine paprika, Italian seasoning, garlic powder and pepper in large resealable food storage bag. Add shrimp; seal bag and shake to coat.

2. Heat oil in large skillet over medium-high heat. Add shrimp; cook 4 minutes or until shrimp are pink and opaque, turning occasionally. Add onion and tomatoes; cook 1 minute or until tomatoes are heated through and onion is softened. Serve with lime wedges, if desired.

MAKES 4 SERVINGS

Easy Chicken Parmesan

1 tablespoon olive oil

4 boneless skinless chicken breasts

1 medium onion, chopped

1 small zucchini, sliced

1 jar (26 ounces) pasta sauce

½ teaspoon dried basil

½ teaspoon dried oregano

8 ounces fresh mozzarella cheese, cut into thin slices

¼ cup grated Parmesan cheese

Hot cooked spaghetti

1. Preheat broiler.

2. Heat oil in large skillet over medium-high heat. Add chicken; cook 5 to 7 minutes or until browned on both sides. Add onion and zucchini; cook 5 minutes or until vegetables are softened. Stir in pasta sauce, basil and oregano. Top chicken with mozzarella slices.

3. Broil 6 inches from heat 5 to 7 minutes or until chicken is no longer pink in center and cheese is beginning to brown. Sprinkle each serving with Parmesan cheese and serve over spaghetti.

MAKES 4 SERVINGS

Grilled 3-Cheese Sandwiches

2 slices (1 ounce each) Muenster cheese

2 slices (1 ounce each) Swiss cheese

2 slices (1 ounce each) Cheddar cheese

2 teaspoons Dijon mustard or Dijon mustard mayonnaise

4 slices sourdough bread

2 teaspoons melted butter

1. Place 1 slice of each cheese on 2 bread slices. Spread mustard over cheese; top with remaining bread slices. Brush outsides of sandwiches with butter.

2. Heat large skillet over medium heat. Add sandwiches; press down lightly with spatula or weigh down with small plate. Cook 4 minutes per side or until cheese is melted and sandwiches are golden brown.

MAKES 2 SANDWICHES

Mexican Mongolian Beef

⅓ cup ORTEGA® Taco Sauce, any variety

⅓ cup hoisin sauce

1 teaspoon ground ginger

1 pound sirloin steak

1 tablespoon cornstarch

2 tablespoons olive oil

1 large onion, sliced

1 to 2 cups cooked vegetables, such as carrots, broccoli or green beans (optional)

Hot cooked rice

4 green onions, sliced

1 tablespoon sesame seeds

COMBINE taco sauce, hoisin sauce and ginger in small bowl; mix well. Set aside.

CUT steak diagonally against the grain into thin slices. Place in medium bowl; toss with cornstarch until evenly coated.

HEAT oil in large skillet over medium heat until hot. Add onion; cook and stir 3 to 4 minutes or until onion is translucent.

ADD steak; cook and stir 5 minutes or until meat is browned. Add sauce mixture and vegetables, if desired; cook and stir 2 minutes or until heated through.

SERVE over rice. Top evenly with green onions and sesame seeds.

MAKES 4 SERVINGS

Tip: For more savory flavor, mix any variety of ORTEGA® Original Salsa into the cooked rice before serving with the dish.

Sassy Chicken & Peppers

- 2 teaspoons Mexican seasoning*
- 2 boneless skinless chicken breasts (about ¼ pound each)
- 2 teaspoons vegetable oil
- 1 small red onion, sliced
- ½ medium red bell pepper, cut into thin strips
- ½ medium yellow or green bell pepper, cut into thin strips

- ¼ cup chunky salsa or chipotle salsa
- 1 tablespoon lime juice
- Lime wedges (optional)

*If Mexican seasoning is not available, substitute 1 teaspoon chili powder, ½ teaspoon ground cumin, ½ teaspoon salt and ⅛ teaspoon ground red pepper.

1. Sprinkle seasoning over both sides of chicken; set aside.

2. Heat oil in large skillet over medium heat. Add onion; cook 3 minutes, stirring occasionally.

3. Add bell peppers; cook 3 minutes, stirring occasionally. Stir salsa and lime juice into vegetables.

4. Push vegetables to edge of skillet. Add chicken to skillet. Cook 5 minutes; turn. Continue to cook 4 minutes or until chicken is no longer pink in center and vegetables are tender.

5. Transfer chicken to serving plates; top with vegetable mixture. Garnish with lime wedges.

MAKES 2 SERVINGS

Crispy Buttermilk Fried Chicken

2 cups buttermilk

1 tablespoon hot pepper sauce

3 pounds bone-in chicken pieces

2 cups all-purpose flour

2 teaspoons salt

2 teaspoons poultry seasoning

1 teaspoon garlic salt

1 teaspoon paprika

1 teaspoon ground red pepper

1 teaspoon black pepper

1 cup vegetable oil

1. Combine buttermilk and hot pepper sauce in large resealable food storage bag. Add chicken; seal bag. Turn to coat; refrigerate 2 hours or up to 24 hours.

2. Combine flour, salt, poultry seasoning, garlic salt, paprika, ground red pepper and black pepper in another large resealable food storage bag or shallow baking dish; blend well. Working in batches, remove chicken from buttermilk; shake off excess. Add to flour mixture; shake to coat.

3. Heat oil over medium heat in large skillet until deep-fry thermometer registers 350°F. Working in batches, fry chicken 30 minutes or until cooked through (165°F), turning occasionally to brown all sides. Drain on paper towels.

MAKES 4 SERVINGS

Note: Carefully monitor the temperature of the oil during cooking. It should not drop below 325°F or go higher than 350°F. The chicken can also be cooked in a deep fryer following the manufacturer's directions. Never leave hot oil unattended.

SIZZLING SIDE DISHES

Tangy Red Cabbage with Apples and Bacon

8 slices thick-cut bacon

1 large onion, sliced

½ small head red cabbage (1 pound), thinly sliced

1 tablespoon sugar

1 Granny Smith apple, peeled and sliced

2 tablespoons cider vinegar

½ teaspoon salt

¼ teaspoon black pepper

1. Heat large skillet over medium-high heat. Add bacon; cook 6 to 8 minutes or until crisp, turning occasionally. Drain on paper towel-lined plate. Coarsely chop bacon.

2. Drain all but 2 tablespoons drippings from skillet. Add onion; cook and stir over medium-high heat 2 to 3 minutes or until onion begins to soften. Add cabbage and sugar; cook and stir 4 to 5 minutes or until cabbage wilts. Stir in apple; cook 3 minutes or until crisp-tender. Stir in vinegar; cook 1 minute or until absorbed.

3. Stir in bacon, salt and pepper; cook 1 minute or until heated through. Serve hot or at room temperature.

MAKES 4 SERVINGS

Charred Corn Salad

3 tablespoons fresh lime juice

½ teaspoon salt

¼ cup extra virgin olive oil

4 to 6 ears corn, husked (enough to make 3 to 4 cups kernels)

⅔ cup canned black beans, rinsed and drained

½ cup chopped fresh cilantro

2 teaspoons minced seeded chipotle pepper (1 canned chipotle pepper in adobo sauce *or* 1 dried chipotle pepper, reconstituted in boiling water)*

Chipotle peppers can sting and irritate the skin, so wear rubber gloves when handling peppers and do not touch your eyes.

1. Whisk lime juice and salt in small bowl. Gradually whisk in oil. Set aside.

2. Heat large skillet over medium-high heat. Cook corn in single layer 15 to 17 minutes or until browned and tender, turning frequently. Transfer to plate to cool slightly. Place in medium bowl.

3. Microwave beans in small microwavable bowl on HIGH 1 minute or until heated through. Add beans, cilantro and chipotle pepper to corn; mix well. Pour lime juice mixture over corn mixture; toss to combine.

MAKES 6 SERVINGS

Note: Chipotle peppers in adobo sauce are available canned in the Mexican food section of most supermarkets. Since only a small amount is needed for this dish, spoon leftovers into a covered plastic container and refrigerate or freeze.

Cantonese Rice Cake Patties

2 cups cooked rice, chilled

⅓ cup chopped red bell pepper

¼ cup thinly sliced green onions

2 egg whites, lightly beaten

1 egg, lightly beaten

2 tablespoons soy sauce

2 tablespoons vegetable oil

1. Combine rice, bell pepper, green onions, egg whites, egg and soy sauce in medium bowl; mix well.

2. Heat 1 tablespoon oil in large skillet over medium heat. Spoon ⅓ cupfuls rice mixture into skillet; flatten slightly with back of spatula. Cook 3 to 4 minutes per side or until golden brown.* Repeat with remaining 1 tablespoon oil and rice mixture.

To keep warm while preparing remaining patties, place on large baking sheet in 200°F oven.

MAKES ABOUT 9 PATTIES

Caramelized Brussels Sprouts with Cranberries

1 tablespoon vegetable oil

1 pound Brussels sprouts, ends trimmed and discarded, thinly sliced

¼ cup dried cranberries

2 teaspoons packed brown sugar

¼ teaspoon salt

Heat oil in large skillet over medium-high heat. Add Brussels sprouts; cook and stir 10 minutes or until crisp-tender and beginning to brown. Add cranberries, brown sugar and salt; cook and stir 5 minutes or until browned.

MAKES 4 SERVINGS

Fried Green Tomatoes

2 medium green tomatoes
¼ cup all-purpose flour
¼ cup yellow cornmeal
½ teaspoon salt
½ teaspoon garlic salt
½ teaspoon ground red pepper

½ teaspoon cracked black pepper
1 cup buttermilk
1 cup vegetable oil
Hot pepper sauce (optional)

1. Cut tomatoes into ¼-inch-thick slices. Combine flour, cornmeal, salt, garlic salt, ground red pepper and black pepper in pie plate or shallow bowl; mix well. Pour buttermilk into second pie plate or shallow bowl.

2. Heat oil in large skillet over medium heat. Dip tomato slices into buttermilk, coating both sides. Immediately dredge slices in flour mixture; shake off excess flour mixture.

3. Cook tomato slices in hot oil 3 to 5 minutes per side. Transfer to paper towels. Serve immediately with hot pepper sauce, if desired.

MAKES 3 TO 4 SERVINGS

Serving Suggestion: Serve fried green tomatoes on a bed of shredded lettuce.

Chinese Vegetables

1 pound fresh broccoli

1½ teaspoons vegetable oil

2 medium yellow onions, cut into wedges and separated

2 cloves garlic, minced

1½ tablespoons minced fresh ginger

8 ounces fresh spinach, coarsely chopped

4 stalks celery, diagonally cut into ½-inch pieces

8 ounces fresh snow peas *or* 1 package (6 ounces) thawed frozen snow peas, trimmed and strings removed

4 medium carrots, sliced

8 green onions, diagonally cut into thin slices

¾ cup chicken broth

1 tablespoon soy sauce

Hot cooked rice

1. Cut broccoli tops into florets. Cut stalks into 2×¼-inch strips.

2. Heat oil in large skillet over high heat. Add broccoli stalks, yellow onions, garlic and ginger; stir-fry 1 minute. Add broccoli florets, spinach, celery, snow peas, carrots and green onions; toss lightly.

3. Add broth and soy sauce to vegetables; toss to coat. Bring to a boil; cover and cook 2 to 3 minutes or until vegetables are crisp-tender. Serve over rice.

MAKES 6 TO 8 SIDE-DISH SERVINGS

Dry-Cooked Green Beans

4 ounces lean ground pork or turkey

2 tablespoons plus 1 teaspoon light soy sauce, divided

2 tablespoons plus 1 teaspoon rice wine or dry sherry, divided

½ teaspoon dark sesame oil

2 tablespoons water

1 teaspoon sugar

3 cups vegetable oil

1 pound fresh green beans, trimmed and cut into 2-inch lengths

1 tablespoon sliced green onion

1. Combine pork, 1 teaspoon soy sauce, 1 teaspoon rice wine and sesame oil in medium bowl; mix well. Set aside.

2. Combine water, sugar, remaining 2 tablespoons soy sauce and 2 tablespoons rice wine in small bowl; mix well. Set aside.

3. Heat vegetable oil in large skillet over medium-high heat until oil registers 375°F on deep-fry thermometer. Carefully add ½ of beans and fry 2 to 3 minutes or until beans blister and are crisp-tender. Remove beans with slotted spoon to paper towels; drain. When oil returns to 375°F, repeat with remaining beans.

4. Pour off oil; heat skillet over medium-high heat 30 seconds. Add pork mixture and stir-fry about 2 minutes or until well browned. Add beans and soy sauce mixture; toss until heated through. Transfer to serving dish. Sprinkle with green onion.

MAKES 4 SERVINGS

Southern-Style Succotash

2 tablespoons butter

1 cup chopped onion

1 package (10 ounces) frozen lima beans, thawed

1 cup frozen corn, thawed

½ cup chopped red bell pepper

1 can (about 15 ounces) hominy, rinsed and drained

⅓ cup chicken broth

¼ teaspoon hot pepper sauce

¼ cup chopped green onion tops or fresh chives

1. Melt butter in large skillet over medium heat. Add onion; cook and stir 5 minutes. Add lima beans, corn and bell pepper; cook and stir 5 minutes.

2. Add hominy, broth and hot pepper sauce; simmer 5 minutes or until most liquid is evaporated. Remove from heat; stir in chopped green onions before serving.

MAKES 6 SERVINGS

Spanish Stewed Tomatoes

2 tablespoons olive oil

½ teaspoon POLANER® Chopped Garlic

1 can (about 15 ounces) diced tomatoes

½ cup water

1 packet (1.25 ounces) ORTEGA® Taco Seasoning Mix

2 cups frozen green beans

2 tablespoons ORTEGA® Fire-Roasted Diced Green Chiles

HEAT oil in medium skillet over medium heat until hot. Add garlic. Cook and stir until golden brown. Stir in tomatoes, water and taco seasoning mix. Simmer 3 minutes. Add beans and chiles; simmer 4 minutes or until beans are heated through.

MAKES 6 SERVINGS

Variation: Replace the green beans with corn or lima beans.

Sesame Snow Peas

½ pound snow peas (Chinese pea pods)

2 teaspoons dark sesame oil

2 teaspoons vegetable oil

1 medium carrot, cut into matchstick pieces

2 green onions, cut into ¼-inch slices

½ teaspoon grated fresh ginger *or* ¼ teaspoon ground ginger

1 teaspoon soy sauce

1 tablespoon sesame seeds, toasted*

To toast sesame seeds, heat small skillet over medium heat. Add sesame seeds; cook and stir about 5 minutes or until golden.

1. To de-stem peas, pinch off stem end from each pod and pull strings down pod to remove, if present. (Young tender pods may have no strings.)

2. To stir-fry, place large skillet over high heat. Add sesame and vegetable oils; heat oil 30 seconds. Add snow peas, carrot, green onions and ginger; stir-fry 4 minutes or until peas are bright green and crisp-tender.

3. Stir in soy sauce. Transfer to warm serving dish; sprinkle with sesame seeds. Serve immediately.

MAKES 4 SIDE-DISH SERVINGS

Asparagus with No-Cook Creamy Mustard Sauce

2 cups water

1½ pounds asparagus, trimmed

½ cup plain yogurt

2 tablespoons mayonnaise

1 tablespoon Dijon mustard

2 teaspoons lemon juice

½ teaspoon salt

Grated lemon peel (optional)

1. Bring water to a boil in large skillet over high heat. Add asparagus; return to a boil. Reduce heat; cover and simmer 3 minutes or until crisp-tender. Drain.

2. Meanwhile, whisk yogurt, mayonnaise, mustard, lemon juice and salt in small bowl until smooth and well blended.

3. Place asparagus on serving platter; top with sauce. Garnish with lemon peel.

MAKES 6 SERVINGS

Creamy Corn and Vegetable Orzo

2 tablespoons butter

4 medium green onions, sliced (about ½ cup)

2 cups frozen whole kernel corn

1 package (10 ounces) frozen vegetables (chopped broccoli, peas, sliced carrots **or** cut green beans)

½ of a 16-ounce package rice-shaped pasta (orzo), cooked and drained

1 can (10¾ ounces) CAMPBELL'S® Condensed Cream of Celery Soup (Regular **or** 98% Fat Free)

½ cup water

1. Heat the butter in a 12-inch skillet over medium heat. Add the green onions and cook until tender. Add the corn, vegetables and pasta. Cook and stir for 3 minutes.

2. Stir the soup and water into the skillet. Cook and stir for 5 minutes or until mixture is hot and bubbling. Serve immediately.

MAKES 6 SERVINGS

Skillet Succotash

- 1 teaspoon canola oil
- ½ cup diced onion
- ½ cup diced green bell pepper
- ½ cup diced celery
- ½ teaspoon paprika
- ¾ cup frozen white or yellow corn
- ¾ cup frozen lima beans
- ½ cup canned diced tomatoes
- 1 teaspoon dried parsley flakes *or* 1 tablespoon minced fresh parsley
- ¼ teaspoon salt
- ¼ teaspoon black pepper

1. Heat oil in large skillet over medium heat. Add onion, bell pepper and celery; cook and stir 5 minutes or until onion is translucent and pepper and celery are crisp-tender. Stir in paprika.

2. Add corn, lima beans and tomatoes. Reduce heat. Cover and simmer 20 minutes or until beans are tender. Stir in parsley, salt and black pepper just before serving.

MAKES 4 SERVINGS

Tip: For additional flavor, add 1 clove minced garlic and 1 bay leaf. Remove and discard bay leaf before serving.

Green Beans and Shiitake Mushrooms

10 to 12 dried shiitake mushrooms (about 1 ounce)

¾ cup water, divided

3 tablespoons oyster sauce

1 tablespoon cornstarch

4 cloves garlic, minced

⅛ teaspoon red pepper flakes

1 tablespoon vegetable oil

¾ to 1 pound fresh green beans, ends trimmed

⅓ cup slivered fresh basil or chopped fresh cilantro

2 green onions, sliced diagonally

⅓ cup roasted peanuts

1. Place mushrooms in bowl; cover with hot water. Let stand 30 minutes or until caps are soft. Drain mushrooms; squeeze out excess water. Remove and discard stems. Slice caps into thin strips.

2. Combine ¼ cup water, oyster sauce, cornstarch, garlic and red pepper flakes in small bowl; mix well. Set aside.

3. Heat oil in medium skillet over medium-high heat. Add mushrooms, beans and remaining ½ cup water; cook and stir until water boils. Reduce heat to medium-low; cover and cook 8 to 10 minutes or until beans are crisp-tender, stirring occasionally.

4. Stir cornstarch mixture; add to skillet. Cook and stir until sauce thickens and coats beans. (If cooking water has evaporated, add enough water to form thick sauce.) Stir in basil, green onions and peanuts; mix well. Transfer to serving platter.

MAKES 4 TO 6 SERVINGS

DELICIOUS DESSERTS

Sautéed Apples Supreme

2 small apples *or* 1 large
   apple

1 teaspoon butter

¼ cup unsweetened apple
   juice or cider

2 teaspoons packed
   brown sugar

½ teaspoon ground
   cinnamon

Vanilla ice cream

2 tablespoons chopped
   walnuts, toasted*

*To toast walnuts, spread in single layer in skillet. Cook and stir over medium heat 1 to 2 minutes or until nuts are lightly browned.

1. Cut apples into quarters; remove cores and cut into ½-inch-thick slices.

2. Melt butter in large skillet over medium heat. Add apples; cook 4 minutes, stirring occasionally.

3. Combine apple juice, brown sugar and cinnamon in small bowl; pour over apples. Simmer 5 minutes or until apples are tender and sauce thickens. Serve over ice cream; sprinkle with walnuts.

MAKES 2 SERVINGS

Cinnamon Dessert Tacos with Fruit Salsa

1 cup sliced fresh strawberries

1 cup cubed fresh pineapple

1 cup cubed peeled kiwi

½ teaspoon minced jalapeno pepper* (optional)

4 tablespoons sugar, divided

1 tablespoon ground cinnamon

6 (8-inch) flour tortillas

Nonstick cooking spray

*Jalapeno peppers can sting and irritate the skin, so wear rubber gloves when handling peppers and do not touch your eyes.

1. Stir together strawberries, pineapple, kiwi, jalapeño pepper and 1 tablespoon sugar in large bowl; set aside. Combine remaining 3 tablespoons sugar and cinnamon in small bowl; set aside.

2. Spray tortilla lightly on both sides with cooking spray. Heat over medium heat in medium skillet until slightly puffed and golden brown. Remove from heat; immediately dust both sides with cinnamon-sugar mixture. Shake excess cinnamon-sugar back into bowl. Repeat until all tortillas are warmed.

3. Fill tortillas with fruit mixture; fold in half. Serve immediately.

MAKES 6 SERVINGS

Poached Pears in Cinnamon-Apricot Sauce

1 can (5½ ounces) apricot nectar

1 tablespoon sugar

1 teaspoon lemon juice

½ teaspoon ground cinnamon

¼ teaspoon grated lemon peel

⅛ teaspoon ground cloves

2 large pears

Whipped topping (optional)

1. Combine apricot nectar, sugar, lemon juice, cinnamon, lemon peel and cloves in large skillet. Bring to a boil over medium-high heat.

2. Meanwhile, cut pears lengthwise into halves, leaving stem attached to one half. Remove cores. Cut pears lengthwise into thin slices, taking care not to cut through stem end. Add pears to skillet with nectar mixture; return to a boil. Reduce heat to medium-low. Simmer, covered, 6 to 8 minutes or just until pears are tender. Carefully remove pears from skillet, reserving liquid.

3. Simmer liquid in skillet, uncovered, over medium heat 2 to 3 minutes or until mixture thickens slightly, stirring occasionally. Fan out pears; spoon sauce over pears. Serve pears warm or chilled with whipped topping, if desired.

MAKES 4 SERVINGS

Chocolate Chip Skillet Cookie

1¾ cups all-purpose flour

1 teaspoon baking soda

1 teaspoon salt

¾ cup (1½ sticks) butter, softened

¾ cup packed brown sugar

½ cup granulated sugar

2 eggs

1 teaspoon vanilla

1 package (12 ounces) semisweet chocolate chips

Sea salt (optional)

Ice cream (optional)

1. Preheat oven to 350°F.

2. Combine flour, baking soda and salt in medium bowl. Beat butter, brown sugar and granulated sugar in large bowl with electric mixer at medium speed until creamy. Beat in eggs and vanilla until well blended. Gradually beat in flour mixture at low speed just until blended. Stir in chocolate chips. Press batter evenly into large skillet. Sprinkle lightly with sea salt, if desired.

3. Bake 35 minutes or until top and edges are golden brown but cookie is still soft in center. Cool on wire rack 10 minutes before cutting into wedges. Serve warm with ice cream, if desired.

MAKES 8 SERVINGS

So-Easy Peach Pie

1 refrigerated pie crust (half of 15-ounce package)

1 package (16 ounces) frozen unsweetened peach slices, thawed, juice reserved

2 teaspoons cornstarch

½ cup golden raisins

4 tablespoons sugar, divided

1 teaspoon vanilla or almond extract

¼ teaspoon ground cinnamon (optional)

1. Let crust stand at room temperature 15 minutes. Preheat oven to 450°F. Spray large baking sheet with nonstick cooking spray or line with parchment paper.

2. Unroll crust on prepared baking sheet; roll or flute edge, if desired. Prick holes in crust several times with fork. Bake 10 to 12 minutes or until golden brown.

3. Meanwhile, combine peach juice and cornstarch in large skillet; stir until cornstarch is dissolved. Add peaches and raisins; bring to a boil over high heat. Boil 2 minutes, stirring occasionally. Remove from heat; stir in 3 tablespoons sugar, vanilla and cinnamon, if desired.

4. Slide baked crust over peach mixture in skillet. Sprinkle with remaining 1 tablespoon sugar.

MAKES 8 SERVINGS

Honey Sopaipillas

¼ cup plus 2 teaspoons sugar, divided

½ teaspoon ground cinnamon

2 cups all-purpose flour

½ teaspoon salt

2 teaspoons baking powder

2 tablespoons shortening

¾ cup warm water

Vegetable oil for deep-frying

Honey

1. Combine ¼ cup sugar and cinnamon in small bowl; set aside. Combine remaining 2 teaspoons sugar, flour, salt and baking powder in large bowl. Cut in shortening with pastry blender or two knives until mixture resembles fine crumbs. Gradually add water; stir with fork until mixture forms dough. Turn out onto lightly floured surface; knead 2 minutes or until smooth. Shape into a ball; cover with bowl and let rest 30 minutes.

2. Divide dough into four equal portions; shape each into a ball. Flatten each ball into 8-inch circle ⅛ inch thick. Cut each round into four wedges.

3. Pour oil into large skillet to depth of 1½ inches. Heat to 360°F. Cook dough, two pieces at a time, 2 minutes or until puffed and golden brown, turning once during cooking. Remove from oil with slotted spoon; drain on paper towels. Sprinkle with cinnamon-sugar mixture. Repeat with remaining sopaipillas. Serve hot with honey.

MAKES 16 SOPAIPILLAS

Sweet and Spicy Bananas Foster

½ cup (1 stick) butter

½ cup firmly packed light brown sugar

2 tablespoons ORTEGA® Taco Seasoning Mix

4 bananas, peeled, halved and cut in half lengthwise

¼ cup dark rum

Vanilla ice cream

MELT butter in large skillet over medium heat. Stir in brown sugar; cook and stir until smooth and sugar has dissolved. Stir in taco seasoning mix.

ADD banana quarters; swirl around in skillet to coat bananas completely. Add rum; simmer 4 minutes or until alcohol has cooked out.

PLACE ice cream in serving dishes. Arrange 4 banana pieces in each dish; spoon sauce over ice cream and bananas.

MAKES 4 SERVINGS

Serving Suggestion: For a warmer treat, serve this sweet and spicy version of bananas Foster over pound cake or your favorite coffee cake.

Chocolate Crêpes with Strawberry Filling

1 cup all-purpose flour

⅔ cup milk

2 egg whites

1 egg

3 tablespoons sugar

3 tablespoons unsweetened cocoa powder

1 tablespoon butter, melted and cooled

½ teaspoon salt

2 teaspoons canola oil

3 tablespoons strawberry fruit spread

3½ cups sliced fresh or thawed frozen strawberries

½ cup thawed frozen whipped topping

Fresh mint leaves (optional)

1. Combine flour, milk, egg whites, egg, sugar, cocoa, butter and salt in large bowl; whisk until smooth and well blended.

2. Brush medium skillet with ¼ teaspoon oil; heat over medium heat. Pour about ¼ cup batter into center of pan. Immediately pick up pan and swirl to coat with batter. Cook 1 minute or until crêpe is dull on top and edges are dry. Turn and cook 30 seconds. Remove to plate and repeat with remaining oil and batter.

3. Stir strawberry fruit spread in medium bowl until softened. Add strawberries; toss to coat.

4. Spoon about ¼ cup strawberry mixture down center of each crêpe; roll up to enclose filling. Top each serving with 2 tablespoons whipped topping. Garnish with mint.

MAKES 8 CRÊPES (ABOUT 4 SERVINGS)

Apple Cranberry Crumble

4 large apples (about 1⅓ pounds), peeled and cut into ¼-inch slices

2 cups fresh or frozen cranberries

⅓ cup granulated sugar

6 tablespoons all-purpose flour, divided

1 teaspoon apple pie spice, divided

¼ teaspoon salt, divided

½ cup chopped walnuts

¼ cup old-fashioned oats

2 tablespoons packed brown sugar

¼ cup (½ stick) butter, cut into small pieces

1. Preheat oven to 375°F.

2. Combine apples, cranberries, granulated sugar, 2 tablespoons flour, ½ teaspoon apple pie spice and ⅛ teaspoon salt in large bowl; toss to coat. Spoon into medium skillet.

3. Combine remaining 4 tablespoons flour, walnuts, oats, brown sugar, remaining ½ teaspoon apple pie spice and ⅛ teaspoon salt in medium bowl; mix well. Cut in butter with pastry blender or two knives until mixture resembles coarse crumbs. Sprinkle over fruit mixture in skillet.

4. Bake 50 to 60 minutes or until filling is bubbly and topping is lightly browned.

MAKES 4 SERVINGS

Hot Skillet Pineapple Orange Snack Cake

1 can (8 ounces) crushed pineapple in juice, undrained

1 cup orange juice, divided

2 tablespoons firmly packed dark brown sugar

1⅓ cups all-purpose flour

¼ cup granulated sugar

¼ cup powdered nonfat milk

2 teaspoons baking powder

½ teaspoon grated orange peel

3 egg whites

2 tablespoons canola oil

1 teaspoon vanilla

1. Preheat oven to 350°F.

2. Drain pineapple in fine mesh strainer, reserving liquid. Place large skillet over high heat. Add pineapple juice and ½ cup orange juice. Bring to a boil; continue boiling 2½ minutes or until liquid measures ¼ cup. Remove skillet from heat; add brown sugar to measured liquid in skillet. Stir until blended. Using teaspoon, spoon pineapple evenly over brown-sugar mixture. Do not stir; set aside.

3. Combine flour, granulated sugar, powdered milk, baking powder and orange peel in medium bowl; stir to blend. Add remaining ½ cup orange juice, egg whites, oil and vanilla. Using electric mixer, beat on low speed to blend. Increase to medium speed and beat 2 minutes or until smooth. Spoon batter evenly over pineapple mixture in skillet.

4. Bake 30 to 35 minutes or until toothpick inserted in center comes out clean. Place on cooling rack 5 minutes. Loosen edges with knife and place plate over skillet. Invert, scraping any remaining pineapple from skillet and spooning on top of cake. Cut into eight wedges and serve warm.

MAKES 8 SERVINGS

Pear Tortetta

⅓ cup granulated sugar

⅓ cup packed brown sugar

½ teaspoon ground cinnamon

4 medium ripe pears, peeled, cored and cut in half

2 tablespoons lemon juice

3 tablespoons margarine, softened

½ of a 17.3-ounce package PEPPERIDGE FARM® Puff Pastry Sheets (1 sheet), thawed

1. Heat the oven to 425°F. Stir the granulated sugar, brown sugar and cinnamon in a small bowl. Brush the pears with the lemon juice.

2. Spread the margarine in a 10-inch oven-safe skillet. Sprinkle with the sugar mixture. Arrange the pear halves in the skillet, cut-side up, with the tapered end of the pears towards the center of the skillet. Cook over medium heat for 8 minutes or until the sugar mixture is thickened. Remove the skillet from the heat.

3. Unfold the pastry sheet on a lightly floured surface. Roll the pastry sheet into a 13-inch circle. Place the pastry over the pears and tuck in the sides lightly around the pears.

4. Bake for 25 minutes or until the pastry is golden brown. Cool in the skillet on a wire rack for 5 minutes. Carefully invert the tortetta onto a serving plate.

MAKES 8 SERVINGS

Kitchen Tip: When inverting the tortetta, make sure to use oven mitts and hold the skillet and plate firmly together. If any pears stick to the skillet, just remove them and arrange them on the tortetta.

Sweet 'n Easy Fruit Crisp Bowls

2 tablespoons granola with almonds

Nonstick cooking spray

1 red apple (8 ounces), such as Gala, diced into ½-inch pieces

1 tablespoon dried sweetened cranberries

¼ teaspoon apple pie spice or ground cinnamon

1 teaspoon butter

1 teaspoon sugar

¼ teaspoon almond extract

Vanilla ice cream

1. Place granola in small resealable food storage bag and crush lightly to form coarse crumbs. Set aside. Heat large skillet over medium heat; coat with cooking spray. Add apples, cranberries and apple pie spice; cook 4 minutes or until apples are just tender, stirring frequently.

2. Remove from heat, stir in butter, sugar and almond extract. Spoon into two dessert bowls. Sprinkle with granola and spoon ice cream on top. Serve immediately.

MAKES 2 SERVINGS

Note: You may make the apple mixture up to 8 hours in advance and top with granola and ice cream at time of serving. To rewarm crisp, microwave apple mixture (before adding granola and ice cream) 20 to 30 seconds on HIGH or until slightly heated.

Cinnamon Tortilla with Cream Cheese & Strawberries

2 teaspoons sugar

⅛ teaspoon ground cinnamon

1 (6-inch) flour tortilla

Nonstick cooking spray

1 tablespoon cream cheese

⅓ cup fresh strawberry slices

1. Combine sugar and cinnamon in small bowl; mix well. Heat large skillet over medium heat.

2. Lightly spray one side of tortilla with cooking spray; sprinkle with cinnamon mixture.

3. Place tortilla, cinnamon side down, in hot skillet. Cook 2 minutes or until lightly browned. Remove from skillet.

4. Spread uncooked side of tortilla with cream cheese; arrange strawberries down center of tortilla. Roll up tortilla to serve.

MAKES 1 SERVING

Caramelized Pineapple

1 tablespoon butter

2 cups fresh pineapple chunks

3 tablespoons sugar

¾ cup vanilla frozen yogurt

1. Melt butter in large skillet over medium-high heat. Add pineapple and sugar; cook and stir 10 to 12 minutes or until pineapple is golden brown, stirring and turning pineapple occasionally. Cool 5 minutes.

2. Spoon pineapple into four dessert dishes. Top each with frozen yogurt. Serve immediately.

MAKES 4 SERVINGS

Index

Acknowledgments

The publisher would like to thank the companies and organization listed below for the use of their recipes and photographs in this publication.

The Beef Checkoff

Bob Evans®

Butterball® Turkey

Campbell Soup Company

The Coca-Cola Company®

The Golden Grain Company®

Hormel Foods, LLC

Johnsonville Sausage, LLC

Ortega®, A Division of B&G Foods North America, Inc.

METRIC CONVERSION CHART

VOLUME MEASUREMENTS (dry)

1/8 teaspoon = 0.5 mL
1/4 teaspoon = 1 mL
1/2 teaspoon = 2 mL
3/4 teaspoon = 4 mL
1 teaspoon = 5 mL
1 tablespoon = 15 mL
2 tablespoons = 30 mL
1/4 cup = 60 mL
1/3 cup = 75 mL
1/2 cup = 125 mL
2/3 cup = 150 mL
3/4 cup = 175 mL
1 cup = 250 mL
2 cups = 1 pint = 500 mL
3 cups = 750 mL
4 cups = 1 quart = 1 L

VOLUME MEASUREMENTS (fluid)

1 fluid ounce (2 tablespoons) = 30 mL
4 fluid ounces (1/2 cup) = 125 mL
8 fluid ounces (1 cup) = 250 mL
12 fluid ounces (1 1/2 cups) = 375 mL
16 fluid ounces (2 cups) = 500 mL

WEIGHTS (mass)

1/2 ounce = 15 g
1 ounce = 30 g
3 ounces = 90 g
4 ounces = 120 g
8 ounces = 225 g
10 ounces = 285 g
12 ounces = 360 g
16 ounces = 1 pound = 450 g

DIMENSIONS

1/16 inch = 2 mm
1/8 inch = 3 mm
1/4 inch = 6 mm
1/2 inch = 1.5 cm
3/4 inch = 2 cm
1 inch = 2.5 cm

OVEN TEMPERATURES

250°F = 120°C
275°F = 140°C
300°F = 150°C
325°F = 160°C
350°F = 180°C
375°F = 190°C
400°F = 200°C
425°F = 220°C
450°F = 230°C

BAKING PAN SIZES

Utensil	Size in Inches/Quarts	Metric Volume	Size in Centimeters
Baking or Cake Pan (square or rectangular)	8×8×2	2 L	20×20×5
	9×9×2	2.5 L	23×23×5
	12×8×2	3 L	30×20×5
	13×9×2	3.5 L	33×23×5
Loaf Pan	8×4×3	1.5 L	20×10×7
	9×5×3	2 L	23×13×7
Round Layer Cake Pan	8×1½	1.2 L	20×4
	9×1½	1.5 L	23×4
Pie Plate	8×1¼	750 mL	20×3
	9×1¼	1 L	23×3
Baking Dish or Casserole	1 quart	1 L	—
	1½ quart	1.5 L	—
	2 quart	2 L	—